GERMAN COOKING

CONTENTS

Colour Library Books

INTRODUCTION

Beer and bratwurst are traditionally the essence of German gastronomy, but there is certainly more to German cooking than that. There is a flavour to Germany's food that is unlike that of any other country. German cooking has an unmistakable taste that depends on highly flavoured ingredients combined in original ways, with less spice and garlic used than in other European countries.

The German "hausfrau" is economically minded even in today's affluent society. Not every meal contains meat, and the humble potato is used in many interesting ways – combined with apple, pears, grated raw into pancakes or cooked with caraway seeds. The main meal is usually served in the middle of the day and is either a meat dish or a high-protein cheese or lentil dish followed by a sweet or fruit. Supper is kept quite simple; a selection of cold meats, sausages and salads, and a variety of breads and rolls.

The German people are very health-conscious; the old idea of the puffing businessman with the "speckbauch" (bacon belly) is fading fast; although many traditional recipes lean heavily on bacon, dumplings and potatoes, the modern German is well aware of calories and the healthy, balanced diet. On special occasions, however, the traditional meals are still cooked. Perhaps the most famous of these is "sauerkraut", cooked in white wine, cider, beer, champagne or flavoured with Kirsch and served with frankfurters, pickled pork, garlic sausage and new boiled potatoes.

The regional specialities of the country tend to be dictated by what has always been traditionally grown, raised or caught in the area. The most important element of influence in the North is the sea. This is Germany's only coast and it supplies all her sea fish. Germans love fish! They marinate and pickle the prolific herring to produce the world-famous "rollmops", and prepare particularly delicious smoked eel and buckling. The North also boasts two of the most sophisticated cities in Germany: Hamburg and Berlin. Hamburg gave birth to the hamburger, perversely known in Germany as Deutsches Beefsteak. The culinary specialities of Berlin are many; pickled cucumbers, hot plum doughnuts and wonderful cakes.

From the centre of Germany comes the delicious Westphalia ham, comparable to Italy's "prosciutto", especially when served with slices of nutty pumpernickel.

Frankfurt in the East must always be associated with its famous sausage and for its light "green sauce" made from chopped herbs, oil, vinegar and sugar. It is also the home of the potato dumpling, fruit tarts and fragrant honey cakes; and from the influence of its Polish neighbours come beer soup and the delicious carp recipes.

To the South, dumplings give way to tiny "spaetzle" and the famous "Himmel und Erde" – potatoes cooked with apples. The well known "strudel" of Bavaria is often filled with savoury fish or cabbage mixtures as well as the conventional fruit.

German cooking remains strongly regional in character, as is to be expected in a large country which until recently was composed of dozens of independent states. The cuisine is the product of both a healthy, well run agriculture and the good-housekeeping that is a part of the German character.

Lentil Soup with Frankfurters

Goulash Soup

Lentil Soup with Frankfurters

Linsensuppe mit Frankfurter

1 cup dried quick-cooking lentils	1 onion, finely chopped
6 cups water	1 tbsp vegetable oil
2 slices lean bacon, diced	2 tbsp flour
1 leek or green onion, finely chopped	1 tbsp vinegar
	4 frankfurters, thickly sliced
1 large carrot, finely chopped	1 tbsp tomato ketchup
1 celery stalk, chopped	1 tsp salt
	¼ tsp black pepper

Wash the lentils thoroughly. In a 2½-quart saucepan bring 6 cups of water to boil. Add the lentils, bacon, leek or green onion, carrot and celery. Simmer, partially covered, for 30 to 40 minutes.

Meanwhile in a frypan, sauté chopped onion in vegetable oil until soft. Sprinkle flour over onion, and stir. Lower heat, stir constantly, and cook until the flour turns light brown. Do not burn flour. Stir ½ cup of hot lentil soup into the browned flour; beat with a wire whisk until well-blended. Beat in vinegar.

Add contents of frypan to lentil pan and stir together. Cover and simmer for 30 minutes or until lentils are soft. Add the frankfurters and ketchup. Cook to heat frankfurters through. Season with salt and pepper and serve hot garnished with crisp bacon pieces. Makes 4 servings.

Goulash Soup

Gulaschsuppe

	1 tsp paprika
2 cups chopped onion	2 cloves garlic, minced
¼ cup shortening	½ tsp salt
3 green peppers, chopped	6 cups beef broth, canned or homemade
3 tbsps tomato paste	
1 lb lean beaf, cut in 1" cubes	1 tbsp lemon juice
dash red pepper	¼ tsp caraway seeds

Fry oinions in hot fat until transparent. Add green peppers and tomato paste. Cover and simmer 10 minutes. Add meat and remaining ingredients. Simmer about 1½ hours, until meat is tender. (Add cubed potatoes if you like and simmer until potatoes are done.) (Best when served the second day.) Makes 6 servings.

Bread Soup

Brot Suppe

7 slices stale black bread	1 tsp sugar
4 cups broth	salt and pepper
grated lemon rind	2 tbsp butter
cinnamon stick	2 tbsp currants
2 cloves	chopped parsley

Cut bread into small squares. Place in a saucepan with 2 cups broth. Leave to soak. Add lemon rind, cinnamon, cloves, sugar, seasoning and remainder of stock. Cook for 15 minutes. Remove cinnamon stick and liquidise. Return to saucepan, stir in the butter and currants. Simmer until currants are swollen. Serve hot, sprinkled with chopped parsley. Serves 4.

Bread Soup

SOUPS

Two-bean Soup

Cabbage Soup

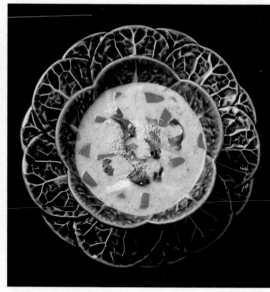

Two-bean Soup

Zwei-bohnensuppe

1¼ cups dry white beans	1 potato, peeled and diced
¼ lb ham, cubed	1 tbsp butter
1 cup cut green beans, fresh or frozen	2 tbsp flour
¼ cup diced celery	¾ cup beef broth
1 green onion, diced	½ tsp salt
1 yellow onion, diced	¼ tsp pepper
	2 sprig parsley for garnish

Cover white beans with cold water and soak overnight. Drain and place beans in a 2-quart saucepan. Add ham and enough cold water to cover beans by 1 inch. Bring water to a boil and simmer for about 1 hour or until beans are tender. Add green beans, celery, onion, and potato. Add enough water to cover the vegetables; simmer for 20 minutes.

In a frypan melt butter and stir in flour. Cook, stirring until lightly browned. Remove from heat and stir in heated beef broth. Cook mixture until smooth. Stir mixture into the soup and simmer until soup is thickened and vegetables are tender. Season with salt and pepper.

Garnish with chopped parsley and serve immediately. Makes 4 to 6 servings.

Cabbage Soup

Krautsuppe

4 thick slices bacon, diced	4 cups chicken stock or bouillon
2 onions, sliced	2 cups water
1 turnip, sliced	6 parsley sprigs and bay leaf tied together with thread
2 carrots, diced	
2 potatoes, cubed	Salt and pepper to taste
1 small head green cabbage, shredded	¼ cup grated Parmesan cheese for garnish

In a 6-quart saucepan or pot, combine all ingredients except salt, pepper and cheese. Simmer partially covered for 1½ to 2 hours. Discard the parsley bundle; season to taste.

Pour into hot soup plates and garnish with cheese. Makes 6 servings.

Chicken Noodle Soup

Hühnerbrühe mit Nudeln

1 chicken weighing about 3 lb	½ cup vermicelli noodles
2 carrots	dried herbs
1 leek	salt and pepper

Joint the chicken. Place in a large pan with cold water just to cover. Add the chopped vegetables. Bring to the boil, add the noodles, 1 tsp dried herbs, salt and pepper. Simmer for a further 15 minutes. Serve at once. Serves 6.

Chicken
Noodle Soup

SOUPS

Potato and Cucumber Soup

Kale and Potato Soup

Potato and Cucumber Soup

Gurken and Kartoffelsuppe

1 medium cucumber	1 cup heavy cream
4 medium potatoes, peeled and diced	1/2 cup milk
1 tsp salt	1 green onion, grated
2 cups cold water	1 tsp dried dillweed (or 1 tbsp chopped fresh dill)
1/4 tsp white pepper	

Peel the cucumber and slice it lengthwise. Scoop out seeds with a spoon and discard. Dice cucumber.

In a heavy 2½-quart saucepan boil potatoes in salted water until the potatoes are very soft. Pour potatoes and cooking liquid into a sieve or food mill set over a large bowl. Force potatoes through. Return to saucepan. Stir in pepper, cream, milk, grated onion and the cucumber. Simmer gently about 5 minutes or until the cucumber is tender.

Add dill and season to taste. Serve hot. Makes 4 servings.

Kale and Potato Soup

Grünkohlsuppe

4 medium potatoes	1/2 tsp pepper
2 tbsp vegetable oil	2 pounds fresh kale
8 cups water	1/2 lb cooked, sliced smoked garlic sausage
1 tsp salt	

Peel and chop potatoes. Combine with vegetable oil and water. Cook for 20 to 30 minutes or until potatoes are tender. Remove potatoes and reserve liquid. Mash potatoes through a sieve and return to potato liquid. Add salt and pepper and simmer for 20 minutes.

Wash kale discarding all tough leaves, and cut into thin shreds. Add to potatoes and cook for 25 minutes.

Add sausage. Simmer gently for 5 minutes. Serve. Make 6 to 8 servings.

Hamburg Fruit Soup

1/2 lb sweet cherries	1/2 lb redcurrants
4 tbsp sugar	1/2 lb bilberries
1/2 lb raspberries	1 tbsp cornstarch
1/2 lb strawberries	

Stone cherries. Reserve a few whole berries. Place remaining fruit in saucepan with sugar and 4 cups water. Simmer until soft. Mix cornstarch with 1 tbsp water. Stir into fruit mixture. Bring to a boil, simmer until thickened. Add more water if necessary. Serve garnished with whole berries. Serves 4.

Hamburg
Fruit Soup

SOUPS

Veal Breast with Herb Stuffing

German Beefsteaks

Veal Breast with Herb Stuffing

Kalbsbrust mit Kräuterfüllung

herb stuffing

3 strips bacon
1 medium onion
1 4-ounce can mushroom
   pieces
¼ cup chopped fresh parsley
1 tbsp chopped fresh dill
1 tbsp dried tarragon leaves
1 tsp dried basil leaves
½ pound lean ground beef
½ cup dried bread crumbs
3 eggs

⅓ cup sour cream
½ tsp salt
¼ tsp pepper

veal

3 to 4 lbs boned veal breast or
   boned leg
½ tsp salt
¼ tsp pepper
1 tbsp vegetable oil
2 cups hot beef broth
2 tbsps cornstarch
½ cup sour cream

To prepare stuffing, dice bacon and onion. Cook bacon in a frypan until partially cooked; add onion and cook for 5 minutes. Drain and chop mushrooms, add to frypan, and cook for another 5 minutes. Remove mixture from heat, let cool, and transfer to a mixing bowl. Add herbs, ground beef, bread crumbs, eggs, and sour cream. Mix thoroughly. Season with salt and pepper.

With a sharp knife, cut a pocket in the veal breast or leg. Fill with stuffing; close opening with toothpicks. (Tie with string if necessary.) Rub outside with salt and pepper.

Heat oil in a Dutch oven. Place meat in the pan and bake in a preheated 350°F oven about 1½ hours. Baste occasionally with beef broth. When done, place meat on a preheated platter.

Pour rest of beef broth into the Dutch oven and scrape brown particles from the bottom. Bring pan drippings to a simmer. Thoroughly blend cornstarch with sour cream and add to pan drippings while stirring. Cook and stir until thick and bubbly.

Slice veal breast and serve sauce separately. Makes 6 servings.

German Beefsteaks

Deutsches Beefsteak

1 large, dry hard roll
½ cup water
4 tbsps vegetable oil
1 medium onion, chopped

1 pound lean ground beef
½ tsp salt
¼ tsp pepper
4 medium onions, sliced

In a small bowl soak roll in water.

Heat 2 tbsps vegetable oil in a frypan; cook chopped onion until lightly browned. Transfer onion to a bowl.

Squeeze roll as dry as possible and mix roll with onions. Add ground beef; blend well. Season with salt and pepper. Shape meat into 4 patties. Heat 2 tbsps vegetable oil in a frypan. Add ground-beef patties; cook about 5 minutes one each side or to desired degree. Remove and keep warm.

Add sliced onions to pan drippings; cook until lightly browned. Arrange beefsteaks on a platter and top with onion rings. Makes 4 servings.

Pork Fillet with Kummel

Schweinefilet mit Kümmel

2 pork tenderloins
2 sticks butter
salt and pepper
4 tsp all purpose flour
2 tbsp oil

8 tbsp brandy
8 tbsp kummel liquer
2 tsp ground caraway seeds
2 tbsp chopped parsley

Sprinkle pork with salt and pepper. Dip in the flour. Saute tenderloins in 1 stick of butter and oil for 20-25 minutes, until just tender but still pink. Keep hot in a warm oven. Add brandy, kummel and remaining butter to the pan. Bring to a boil. Stir in caraway seeds. Slice tenderloins, arrange on a bed of potato puree. Pour the sauce. Garnish with chopped parsley. Serves 6-8.

Pork Fillet
with Kummel

MEATS

Meatballs Königsberg-style*

Bavarian Veal with Asparagus

Meatballs Königsberg-style*

Königsberger Klopse

meatballs	1 bay leaf
1 roll	1 small onion, peeled and
¾ cup water	halved
1 pound lean ground beef	6 peppercorns
1 strip bacon, diced	
4 anchovy fillets, diced	gravy
1 small onion, chopped	1½ tbsps butter or margarine
1 egg	1½ tbsps flour
½ tsp salt	1 tbsp capers
¼ tsp white pepper	juice of ½ lemon
	½ tsp prepared mustard
broth	1 egg yolk
6 cups water	¼ tsp salt
½ tsp salt	¼ tsp white pepper

Soak the roll in the water for about 10 minutes. Squeeze it dry; place in mixing bowl with the ground beef. Add the bacon, anchovy fillets, one egg, salt, and pepper. Mix thoroughly.

Prepare the broth by boiling the water, seasoned with salt, bay leaf, onion, and peppercorns.

Shape the meat mixture into balls about 2 inches in diameter. Add to boiling broth and simmer over low heat for 20 minutes. Remove metablls with a slotted spoon, set aside, and keep warm. Strain the broth through a sieve. Reserve broth and keep warm.

To prepare gravy, heat butter in a frypan and stir in flour. Cook for 3 minutes, stirring constantly. Slowly blend in 2 cups of reserved broth. Add the drained capers, lemon juice, and mustard. Simmer for 5 minutes. Remove a small amount of the sauce to blend with the egg yolk. Stir the yolk back into the sauce. Season with salt and pepper.

Place reserved meatballs into the gravy and reheat if necessary. Serve on a preheated platter. Makes 4 servings.

Pickled Pork with Sauerkraut

Eisbein auf Sauerkraut

2 lbs knuckles of pork	sauerkraut:
1 onion	2 lbs sauerkraut
1 bayleaf	4 tbsp oil
4 tsp salt	2 onions, finely chopped
5 coriander seeds	1 potato, peeled and grated
5 ground black peppercorns	5 juniper berries
	1 cup white wine
	2 tsp sugar

In a saucepan, cover the pork with cold water. Add the onion, bayleaf, salt and spices. Bring to a boil, simmer for 1½ hours.

Roughly chop the sauerkraut. Bring to a boil with 2 cups of pork cooking liquid. Heat the oil in a frying pan, sauté the onions until brown. Add to the sauerkraut with juniper berries and wine. After 40 minutes add potatoes. Mix well. Cook for a further 10 minutes. Add the sugar. Arrange sauerkraut and pork on a serving platter. Serves 6.

Roast Pork with Madeira Sauce

Schweinebraten in Madeirasosse

3 to 4 lb pork roast, boneless	1 tbsp vinegar
Peel from 1 lemon	1 cup dry white wine
2 bay leaves	2 tbsp flour
½ tsp salt	¼ cup Madeira wine
⅛ tsp white pepper	

Place roast in roasting pan. Place lemon peel and bay leaves in bottom of pan. Mix salt, pepper, vinegar, and white wine. Pour over meat, Roast meat 325°F until internal temperature reaches 170°F (about 2 to 2½ hours). Baste meat with pan juices about every ½ hour. When roast is done, remove from pan. Degrease pan juice.

Mix flour with Madeira wine; gradually add to juices, stirring constantly with wire whisk. Cook until gravy thickens. Slice meat and serve with gravy and spaetzle, potatoes, or noddles. Makes 6 to 8 servings.

Roast Pork with Madeira Sauce

MEATS

Veal Cutlets with Cherry Sauce

Marinated Leg of Mutton

Veal Cutlets with Cherry Sauce

Kalbsschnitzel in Kirsch Sosse

4 lean veal cutlets, about 6 ounces each	¼ cup red wine
1 tbsp vegetable oil	2 tbsps evaporated milk
½ tsp salt	1 16-ounce can tart cherries, drained
⅛ tsp white pepper	parsley for garnish

Pat cutlets dry with paper towels. Heat oil in a frypan and brown cutlets on each side approximately 3 minutes. Seaon with salt and pepper. Remove cutlets from pan and keep them warm.

Blend wine and evaporated milk in pan and simmer for 3 minutes. Add cherries; heat through and adjust seasonings. Return cutlets to sauce and heat, but do not boil.

Arrange cutlets on preheated platter, pouring cherry sauce around them. Garnish with parsley. Makes 4 servings.

Marinated Leg of Mutton

Sauerliche Hammelkeule

1 leg lamb, bone removed	Marinade: –
¼ lb bacon, shredded	2 chopped carrots
3 tbsp oil	2 chopped onions
2 cups sour cream	7 cups buttermilk
1 cup soft white breadcrumbs	1 cup vinegar
salt and pepper	1 bayleaf
chopped parsley	1 tsp sugar
chopped chives	12 ground peppercorns
	1 tsp salt

Mix ingredients for marinade in a large earthenware casserole. Place the meat in it and leave for 3 days, turning over every day. Dry the joint, make small incisions into the flesh and insert the bacon pieces. Heat the oil, brown the meat well on all sides. Add 1 cup marinade. Cover and cook for 1½ hours, or until tender. Remove meat, thicken juices by adding breadcrumbs, and sour cream. Finally season with herbs. Cut meat into slices. Pour sauce over it. Serve with roast potatoes or potato salad. Serves 6.

Ragout a la Berghoff

Berghoff Ragout

¾ cup butter	2 cups beef broth, canned or homemade
3½-lb boneless round steak, cut into thin strips	1 cup dry white wine
1 cup chopped onion	1 tsp salt
1½ cup chopped green pepper	1 tsp Worcestershire sauce
1 lb mushrooms, sliced	few drops Tabasco sauce (to taste)
½ cup flour	

Melt ½ cup butter in large frypan. Brown meat over medium-height heat. Remove browned meat.

Sauté onion for 2 minutes in remaining butter. Add green pepper and mushrooms. Cook an additional 3 minutes.

Melt ¼ cup butter and add flour. Slowly add beef broth; cook until thickened. Stir in wine and seasonings. Add meat and mushroom mixture. Cover and simmer 45 minutes to 1 hour, until meat is tender. Serve with cheese noodles or dumplings. Makes 8 servings.

Ragout a la
Berghoff

MEATS

Beef Rolls

Sauerbraten with Gingersnap Gravy

Beef Rolls

Rinderrouladen

The people of Berlin claim the origin of this dish.

4 pieces steak roll or sandwich steaks, each about 6 ounces	2 strips bacon, cut into thin strips
2 tsp Dijon-style mustard	1 large onion, chopped
½ tsp salt	¼ cup vegetable oil
¼ tsp pepper	1½ cups hot beef broth
2 large pickles, cut into long, thin strips	4 peppercorns
	½ bay leaf
	1 tbsp cornstarch

Lay steaks on a flat surface. Spread each with mustard; sprinkle with salt and pepper.

Divide pickles, bacon and onion among the steaks as shown. Roll up steaks jelly-roll fashion; secure with beef-roll clamps, toothpicks, or thread.

Heat oil in a heavy saucepan, add the steak rolls, and brown well on all sides – about 15 minutes. Pour in hot beef broth, peppercorns, and bay leaf. Cover and simmer for 1 hour and 20 minutes. Remove beef rolls, discard clamps, and arrange on a preheated platter.

Blend cornstarch with a small amount of cold water, stir into gravy, and bring to a boil, until thick and bubbly. Correct seasonings and serve separately with potato dumplings. Makes 4 servings.

Sauerbraten with Gingersnap Gravy

Sauerbraten mit Ingwerkuchen sosse

4-pound beef rump roast	½ cup cider vinegar
2 onions, thinly sliced	¼ cup vegetable oil
8 peppercorns	½ tsp salt
4 cloves	2 cups boiling water
1 bay leaf	10 gingersnaps
1 cup mild white vinegar	½ cup sour cream
1 cup water	1 tbsp flour

Place the beef roast in a deep ceramic or glass bowl. Add onions, peppercorns, cloves, and bay leaf. Pour white vinegar, water, and cider vinegar over the meat; chill, covered, for 4 days. Turn meat twice each day.

Remove the meat from the marinade, dry it well with paper towels, and strain the marinade into a bowl. Reserve the onions and 1 cup of marinade.

In a Dutch oven brown the meat on all sides in hot vegetable oil. Sprinkle meat with salt. Pour boiling water around the meat, sprinkle in crushed gingersnaps, and simmer, covered, for 1½ hours. Turn often. Add 1 cup of reserved marinade and cook meat 2 hours or more, until tender. Remove the meat and keep it warm. Strain the cooking juices into a large saucepan.

In a small bowl mix sour cream with flour. Stir it into the cooking juices and cook, stirring, until sauce is thickened and smooth. Slice the meat into ¼-inch slices; add to the hot gravy.

Arrange meat on a heated platter and pour extra sauce over it. Makes 8 to 10 servings.

Bavarian Veal with Asparagus

MEATS

Bavarian Veal with Asparagus

Bayerisches Kalbfleisch mit Sparge

2 pounds veal cubes
2 tbsps vegetable oil
1 large onion, chopped
1 cup chopped carrots
1 tbsp chopped parsley
¼ cup fresh lemon juice
2 cups beef broth

3 tbsps flour
½ tsp salt
freshly ground pepper to
    taste
2 pounds fresh, cleaned and
    cut into 1 inch pieces

In a Dutch oven brown the veal in hot oil. Add onion and carrots. Cook until onion is transparent. Stir in parsley.

Mix lemon juice, broth, flour, and seasonings until well-blended. Pour over meat. Cover and bake in preheated 325°F oven 1½ hours or until meat is tender. Add more broth, if needed.

Cook asparagus until tender-crisp. Stir into veal and serve immediately. Makes 6 servings.

Goose

Chicken Peasant Style

Goose

Gans

1 large goose	1 large onion
apples	

Stuff the inside of the cleaned goose with cored apples. Sew up the goose and place on a rack over a large baking pan, breast side down. Pour over half a pint of boiling water. Add the chopped onion to the pan. Cook at 350°F for 40 minutes. Remove from oven, turn the goose breast side up. Baste with the pan juices. Roast for a further 2 hours. Thicken pan juices to make a gravy. Strain, and season. Serve with parsley, potatoes and red cabbage.

Chicken Peasant Style

Jünges Huhn nach Bauernart

1 chicken about 3 lb	½ cup mushrooms
1 egg, beaten	lemon juice
soft white breadcrumbs	½ stick butter
grated Parmesan cheese	1 cup Bechamel sauce
½ cup white wine	salt and pepper

Joint the chicken. Mix the cheese and breadcrumbs together. Coat the chicken pieces in the egg then the breadcrumb mixture. Fry in butter until brown and tender. Remove from the pan, set aside. Fry the mushrooms for 2-3 min, add the sauce, season and add 1 tsp lemon juice. Stir well and add the white wine. Pour the sauce over the chicken, serve with potato salad and a crisp green salad. Serves 4-6.

Black Forest Stew

Schwarzwälder Eintopf

marinade	
1 cup chopped onions	3 cups dry red wine
½ cup chopped carrot	¼ cup red wine vinegar
½ cup chopped celery	½ cup vegetable oil
1 clove garlic, minced	
2 whole cloves	stew
¼ tsp rosemary	3 lbs venison stew meat
¼ tsp thyme	½ tsp marjoram
1 bay leaf	¼ cup butter or margarine
6 cranberries	1 cup chopped onions
5 peppercorns	¼ cup flour
1 tbsp chopped parsley	1 cup beef broth
½ tsp salt	¼ tsp pepper
	1 cup sour cream

Place marinade ingredients into a 2-quart saucepan. Bring marinade to a boil. Reduce heat and simmer 10 minutes. Cool. Place venison and marjoram in a large casserole. Pour cooled marinade over meat. Cover and refrigerate for 24 hours, stirring occasionally. Drain meat, reserving marinade. Pat meat dry.

In a large saucepan melt the butter. When hot, add the meat; brown, stirring to prevent burning. Remove meat and brown remaining 1 cup onions. Stir in flour; mix until well-blended. Add broth and 2 cups reserved marinade. Add pepper. Bring stew to a boil, stirring until slightly thickened. Add meat, cover, and simmer about 1 hour, until meat is tender. Skim off fat. Add sour cream and heat through. Makes 8 servings.

Black
Forest Stew

POULTRY

Grandma's Chicken

Hunter's Chicken

Grandma's Chicken

Hähnchen auf Grossmutterart

2 very small chickens	6 medium potatoes
¼ cup vegetable oil	4 slices bacon
1 tsp salt	4 to 6 small onions
½ tsp white pepper	¼ cup hot beef bouillon
2 tsp paprika	Parsley sprigs for garnish

Clean chickens. Heat oil in a large Dutch oven. Add chickens; brown well on all sides for about 10 minutes. Season with salt, white pepper, and paprika. Continue cooking for another 10 minutes, turning often.

Meanwhile, peel potatoes and cut into 1-inch cubes. Cut bacon into 1-inch pieces. Add potatoes and bacon to chicken. Cook for 5 minutes.

Dice onions and stir in with hot beef bouillon. Cook and bake in a preheated 350°F oven about 45 minutes. Remove cover and bake another 5 minutes to brown the chicken. Arrange on a preheated platter and garnish with parsley. Makes 4 servings.

Hunter's Chicken

Junges Huhn nach Jägerart

1 chicken, weighing about	½ cup mushrooms
2½-3 lb	2 large onions
2 tbsp olive oil	mixed dried herbs
1 small glass brandy	1 tbsp tomato paste

Joint the chicken. Sauté in the oil until well browned and tender, about 25 minutes. Remove from the pan and reserve. Keep warm. In the same pan, sauté the sliced mushrooms and chopped onions. Add the tomato paste, herbs and brandy. Cook for 2-4 minutes then pour over the chicken. Serve with a green salad and boiled noodles with poppy seeds.

Chicken Livers with Apples and Onion

Hühnerleber mit Äpfeln und Zwiebeln

¾ pound chicken livers	3 medium apples
3 tbsps flour	¼ cup vegetable oil
½ tsp salt	¼ cup sugar
¼ tsp pepper	1 large onion, thinly sliced
⅛ tsp cayenne pepper	

Rinse chicken livers and drain on paper towels. Coat livers evenly with a mixture of flour, salt, pepper, and cayenne pepper. Set aside.

Wash and remove cores from apples. Cut apples into ½-inch slices, to form rings.

Heat 2 tbsps vegetable oil in a fryingpan over medium heat. Add sliced apples and cook until lightly brown. Turn slices carefully and sprinkle with sugar. Cook uncovered over low heat until tender. Remove from pan and reserve.

Heat remaining 2 tbsps vegetable oil over low heat. Add chicken livers and onion rings. Cook over medium heat, turning mixture often to brown all sides. Transfer to a warm serving platter.

Serve with apple rings. Makes 4 servings.

Chicken Livers with Apples and Onion

POULTRY

Marinated Rabbit

Marinated Rabbit

Marinierter Hase

1 3-lb rabbit, cut into serving
   pieces
1 tsp salt
¼ tsp pepper
3 tbsp vegetable oil

marinade
2 cups red wine
2 cups chicken broth
1 tsp allspice

2 bay leaves
1 tsp thyme

sauce
1 dozen pickled white onions
   (cocktail size)
1 dozen stuffed green olives,
   sliced
½ lb fresh mushrooms, sliced
2 tbsp butter

Rub rabbit with salt and pepper; put into a large bowl.
Mix together marinade ingredients, add to rabbit, and
refrigerate overnight. Drain the pieces of rabbit, but do
not pat dry. Strain and reserve the marinade.

In a large frypan over high heat, quickly brown all
sides of rabbit pieces in hot vegetable oil. When brown,
pour in reserved marinade and simmer over low heat 1
hour or until rabbit is tender.

Just before rabbit is done, sauté onions, olives, and
mushrooms in hot butter. Add to rabbit mixture. Serve
with boiled potatoes. Makes 6 servings.

Partridges
with Sauerkraut

GAME

Partridges with Sauerkraut

Rebhühner mit Sauerkraut

2 large partridges
salt and pepper
6 slices bacon
2 sticks butter

1 cup beef broth
1 small chopped onion
2 lbs sauerkraut
5 juniper berries

Clean partridges. Rub inside and out with salt and pepper. Cover with bacon slices. Heat the butter in a large saucepan. Brown partridges well on all sides for 10 minutes. Add onion, juniper berries and broth. Cover and simmer for about 1 hour or until tender. Baste with liquid 2 or 3 times during cooking. Cook the sauerkraut, joint the birds. Arrange on a heated platter with the bacon. Serves 4.

Blue Trout

Herring Salad Elbe

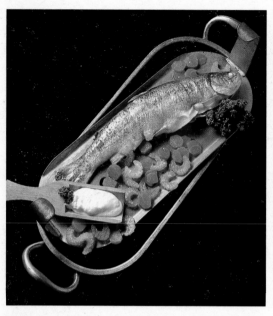

Blue Trout

Forelle blau

4 ³/₄-lb freshwater trout (eviscerated only)	¹/₄ cup white wine
	1 sprig parsley for garnish
2 tsps salt	1 lemon for garnish
1 cup vinegar, heated	1 tomato for garnish
4 cups water	

Rinse fish thoroughly with cold water. Sprinkle ¹/₄ tsp salt inside each fish. To make the trout look attractive, tie a thread through the tail and the underside of the mouth to form a ring (see picture). Arrange fish on a large platter and pour hot vinegar over them. This process will turn them blue in colour.

In a 4-quart saucepot bring water, remaining salt, and wine to a simmer. Carefully place the trout in the water and simmer (be sure not to boil) about 15 minutes. Remove trout with a slotted spoon, drain on paper towels, and arrange on a preheated platter. Garnish with parsley, lemon, and tomato slices. Makes 4 servings.

In Germany, fresh water trout is served with small boiled potatoes that have been tossed in melted butter and sprinkled with chopped parsley. A cold sauce accompanies the dish. This is made from 1 cup whipped heavy cream, ¹/₄ tsp sugar, 2 tbsps prepared horseradish, 1 tsp lemon juice, and salt and pepper to taste.

Herring Salad Elbe

Heringssalat Elbe

4 herring fillets	2 tbsp mayonnaise
2 apples	2 tbsp sour cream
2 dill gherkins	salt and pepper
1 medium onion	

Soak herrings in cold water for 24 hours. Mix the herrings, chopped apple, chopped gherkin and onion together. Arrange on a serving platter. Beat the mayonnaise with the sour cream and seasoning. Spoon over the herring mixture. Garnish with apples and chopped dill. Can be served with slices of rye bread and butter.

Fish Fricassee

Fischfrikassee

1¹/₂ lbs cooked white fish fillet	¹/₂ cup dry cider
¹/₂ cup sliced mushrooms	2 egg yolks
¹/₄ cup chopped onion	3 tbsp lemon juice
2 tbsp butter	salt and pepper
2 tbsp all purpose flour	capers
2 cups fish broth	

Cut fish into 1 inch pieces. Saute the mushrooms and onion in the butter. Add the flour. Stir in the broth and cider. Bring to a boil. Simmer for 2-3 minutes. Strain. Beat in the egg yolks, lemon juice, salt and pepper. Return to saucepan with the fish. Simmer for 2 minutes to re-heat. Arrange on a serving platter garnished with capers, and shrimps if wished. Serves 4.

Fish
Fricassee

Fish Ragout

Boiled Skate with Onion Butter

Fish Ragout

Fischragout

1 lb cooked white fish fillet	½ stick butter
½ lb mushrooms	¼ cup soft white
2 cups bechamel sauce	breadcrumbs

Cut the fish into 1 inch pieces. Coat in sauce and arrange in a casserole. Slice the mushrooms saute in half the melted butter for 2-4 minutes. Spoon over the fish. Sprinkle with breadcrumbs, and remaining butter. Bake at 350°F for 25 minutes until golden. Serves 4.

Boiled Skate with Onion Butter

Rochen Gekocht mit Zwiebelbutter

2 lbs skate	peppercorns
salt	bayleaves
2 large chopped onions	mixed dried herbs
1 stick butter	3 tbsp lemon juice
1 tbsp chopped parsley	3 cloves

Wash fish. Rub in salt and lemon. Leave for 1 hour. Cover with water, add peppercorns, bayleaves, cloves and herbs. Simmer for 30 minutes. Cool, carefully skin fish. Heat butter, saute onions for 2-3 minutes. Add lemon juice and parsley. Pour over the fish to serve. Serves 4.

Stuffed May Fish

Gefüllter Maifisch

4 mackerel	sprigs parsley
½ cup ground boiled ham	salt
4 tomatoes	½ cup milk
¼ cup soft white	2 tbsp flour
breadcrumbs	2 sticks butter

Clean and salt the insides of the fish. Make a stuffing with the ground ham, chopped tomatoes, breadcrumbs, chopped parsley, salt and milk. Loosely fill fish with mixture. Sew up the open sides. Coat fish in flour. Brown well on all sides in the butter. Place in casserole. Cook at 325°F for 30 minutes. Serve with potato salad. Serves 4.

Stuffed
May Fish

FISH

Herring Cocktail Glückstadt

Cold Salmon with Remoulade Sauce

Herring Cocktail Glückstadt

Heringssalat

4 herring fillets	3 tbsp mayonnaise
2 tart apples	1 tbsp heavy cream
1 medium dill cucumber	2 tsp tomato ketchup
2 medium boiled potatoes	1 tsp curry powder
1 small onion chopped	

Dice the herrings, apples, cucumber and potatoes. Mix together the onion, mayonnaise, cream, ketchup and curry powder. Stir in the herring, apple, cucumber and potatoes.

Serve garnished with rolled herring, fresh dill, pineapple and shredded lettuce.

Cold Salmon with Remoulade Sauce

Kalter Lachs mit remouladen sauce

2 lbs cold cooked salmon	1 tsp chopped chervil
1 cup mayonnaise	1 tsp German mustard
1 tbsp chopped gherkins	1 tbsp chopped anchovies
1 tbsp chopped capers	grated rind of 1 lemon
1 tbsp chopped parsley	

Mix the mayonnaise, gherkins and capers. Leave for 1 hour. Add the chopped parsley, chervil, mustard, chopped anchovies, and lemon rind.

Arrange the salmon on a wooden platter. Garnish with lemon slices, and parsley sprigs. Serve with the remoulade sauce. Serves 4.

Lobster Cooked in Beer

Hummer in Weissbier

1 small cooked lobster	caraway seeds
1½ cups light beer	pepper
1 onion	

Cut lobster in half, lengthwise. Crack legs and claws. Remove sand sack and dark coloured intestine. Remove flesh. Cut into 1 inch dice. Bring beer, chopped onion, pepper and caraway seeds to a boil. Simmer for 2-3 minutes. Strain. Arrange lobster halves on heated serving platter. Pour over the beer sauce. Serves 2.

Lobster
Cooked in Beer

FISH

Cod
Hamburg style

Cod Hamburg style

Kabeljau nach Hamburger art

2 lbs cod	2 tbsp butter
salt, pepper and mace	1 dozen oysters
4 tbsp lemon juice	¼ cup soft white
1 cup white wine	breadcrumbs

Clean fish. Rub with salt and lemon juice. Leave in cold place for 2 hours. Put in a shallow pan with white wine and 1 cup water. Season with salt and pepper and mace. Simmer for 25-30 minutes until tender. Strain off fish. Strain liquid. Heat butter in a frying pan, fry the breadcrumbs and gradually pour in the fish liquid. Add oysters, bring to a boil. Simmer 1 minute. Arrange fish on heated serving platter. Pour over oyster sauce. Garnish with lemon. Serves 4.

Collared Herrings

FISH

Collard Herrings

Rollmops

2 lb fresh herrings
tarragon vinegar
milk
peppercorns
bayleaves

pickled gherkins, chopped
chopped onion
mustard seeds
onion slices

Clean herrings, remove heads and tails. Soak in cold water for 12 hours. Drain. Soak in milk for 12 hours. Fillet the herrings. Put some chopped onion, gherkin and peppercorns in each fillet. Roll up, secure with a tooth-pick. Place in a tall jar with bayleaves, mustard seeds, peppercorns, onion slices and gherkin. Beat herring roes with enough vinegar to cover herrings. Cover and leave for 3-4 days. Serve drained of marinade with slices of brown bread and butter.

Potato Pancakes

Brunswick Castle Salad

Potato Pancakes

Kartoffelpfannkuchen

2 large potatoes (grated on medium grater, makes about 2½ cups)	1 boiled potato, mashed
3 cups water	1 egg, beaten
1 tsp lemon juice	2 tbsps milk
	½ tsp salt
	6 to 8 tbsps vegetable oil

Grate raw potatoes into water to which lemon juice has been added. Place potatoes in a strainer or cheesecloth and drain off liquid well.

Beat raw and cooked potatoes with egg, milk, and salt to form a batter. Using 3 tbsps oil for each batch, drop batter for 3 or 4 pancakes at a time into hot oil in large frypan. When firm on bottom side, loosen edges and turn. Brown other side. Remove, drain on paper towels, and keep warm. Continue until all batter is used. Serve immediately. If potato cakes are served with meat, sprinkle with salt. Sprinkle with sugar if served with apple sauce. Makes 8 to 10 pancakes, or 3 to 4 servings.

Brunswick Castle Salad

Braunschweiger Schloss Salat

1 lb celeriac	2 tbsps mayonnaise
¼ cup truffles	2 hard-cooked eggs
1 tbsp oil	2 tbsps chopped fresh
½ tsp vinegar	tarragon

Cook celeriac. Thinly slice. Arrange on a serving platter with truffles. Pour over oil and vinegar. Add mayonnaise and chopped tarragon. Chill for 30 minutes. Garnish with slices of hard-cooked egg.

Celeriac Salad

Sellerie Salat

2 large celeriac	¼ cup oil
2 medium onions finely chopped	salt and pepper
¼ cup white vinegar	sugar

Cook celeriac. Peel while warm. Cut into ½ inch thick slices. Arrange on a serving platter.

Whisk together the onions, vinegar, oil, salt, pepper and sugar to taste. Pour over celeriac. Leave for several hours. Garnish with chopped parsley, and parsley sprigs.

Celeriac
Salad

VEGETABLES

Hot Potato Salad

Westphalian Cabbage

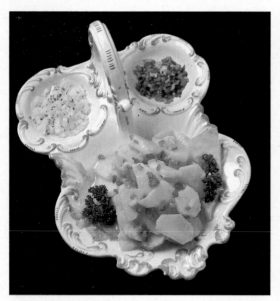

Hot Potato Salad

Warmer Kartoffelsalat

3 medium potatoes, boiled in skins	¾ tsp salt
	¼ tsp celery seeds
3 slices bacon	¼ tsp pepper
¼ cup chopped onion	⅜ cup water
1 tbsp flour	2½ tbsps vinegar
2 tsps sugar	

Peel potatoes and slice thin.

Sauté bacon slowly in a frypan, then drain on paper towels. Sauté onion in bacon fat until golden brown. Blend in flour, sugar, salt, celery seeds, and pepper. Cook over low heat, stirring until smooth and bubbly. Remove from heat. Stir in water and vinegar. Heat to boiling, stirring constantly. Boil for 1 minute. Carefully stir in the potatoes and crumbled bacon bits. Remove from heat, cover, and let stand until ready to serve. Makes 4 servings.

Westphalian Cabbage

Westfälischer/Kohl

1 head cabbage approximately 2 pounds	2 to 3 small tart apples
	1 tbsp cornstarch
3 tbsps vegetable oil	2 tbsps cold water
1 tsp salt	3 tbsps red wine vinegar
1 tsp caraway seeds	¼ tsp sugar
1 cup hot beef broth	

Shred cabbage.

Heat vegetable oil in Dutch oven, add cabbage, and sauté for 5 minutes. Season with salt and caraway seeds. Pour in beef broth, cover, and simmer over low heat about 15 minutes.

Meanwhile, peel, quarter, core, and cut apples into thin wedges. Add the cabbage and simmer for another 30 minutes.

Blend cornstarch with cold water, add to cabbage, and stir until thickened and bubbly.

Season with vinegar and sugar just before serving. Garnish with crisp bacon pieces. Makes 4 to 6 servings.

Heaven and Earth

Himmel und Erde

1 lb peeled quartered potatoes	½ cup diced bacon
1 lb apples	salt and pepper

Cook potatoes in boiling salted water for 10-15 minutes. Add peeled, cored and quartered apples. Season with salt and pepper. Cook for 10 minutes until soft. Beat well until smooth. Fry bacon until crisp, sprinkle over apples and potatoes. Can be served with sliced black puddings.

Heaven
and Earth

VEGETABLES

Stuffed Artichoke Bottoms

Pickelsteiner Casserole

Stuffed Artichoke Bottoms

Artischockenböden Gefüllte

6 globe artichokes	½ cup sliced mushrooms
1 small onion chopped	1 cup bechamel sauce
1 stick butter	grated cheese

Cook artichokes in boiling salted water for 35-40 minutes, or until tender. Remove all leaves and choke. This leaves 'fond' or bottom. Saute onion and mushrooms in the butter. Mix with bechamel sauce. Spoon this mixture onto artichokes. Sprinkle with grated cheese. Bake at 350°F for 20 minutes.

Pickelsteiner Casserole

Pickelsteiner Topf

2 carrots	salt and pepper
2 large potatoes	1 tsp chopped fresh
1 large onion	marjoram, thyme and
1 lb mixed neck of beef, pork and lamb	parsley.

Cut carrots, potatoes, and onions into thin matchstick sized pieces. Cut meat into 1 inch dice. Cover meat with cold water. Bring to a boil. Cover and simmer for 1½ hours. Add vegetables. Cook for a further 10 minutes. Strain well. Arrange on a serving platter. Sprinkle with chopped marjoram, thyme and parsley.

Stuffed Cucumber

Gefüllte Gurken

2 medium cucumbers	salt and pepper
2 slices white sandwich bread	chopped dill
½ lb ground cooked beef	bacon slices
½ cup heavy cream	

Peel the cucumber. With a sharp knife, scoop out a hollow along the length of the cucumber. Cook in boiling water for 2 minutes. Drain well. Soak the bread in cold water, then squeeze dry. Mix with ground beef, dill, salt and pepper. Fill cucumbers with mixture. Wrap slices of bacon round cucumbers. Place in flat casserole. Pour in enough broth to almost cover cucumbers. Bake at 350°F for 1 hour. Drain cucumbers place on heated serving platter. Stir cream into cooking liquid. Pour over cucumbers to serve. Serves 4.

Stuffed
Cucumber

VEGETABLES

Cooked Potato Dumplings

Napkin Dumplings with Pears and Beans

Cooked Potato Dumplings

Gekochte Kartoffelklösse

6 medium potatoes, cooked in skins	crumbs sautéed in ½ cup melted butter or margarine
½ to 1 cup flour	6 to 8 cups hot beef or
2 eggs, beaten	chicken broth
1 tsp salt	½ cup melted butter
1 cup day-old white bread	

Peel and grate potatoes while warm. Blend in flour, eggs, and salt to form a dough stiff enough to shape with fingers. Shape into balls 2 or 3 inches in diameter. If dumplings do not shape well, add more flour to dough. Force a few fried bread crumbs into the centre of each ball; seal over. Reserve rest of crumbs.

Cook dumplings in boiling broth until they rise to the top – about 10 minutes.

Spoon melted butter over tops; sprinkle with remaining fried bread crumbs. Makes 4 to 6 servings – 8 to 12 dumplings, depending on size.

Napkin Dumplings with Pears and Beans

Serviettenklösse mit Birnen und Bohnen

10 slices of white sandwich bread, diced	2 lbs French beans
	¼ cup sugar
½ stick butter	¼ cup diced bacon
3 eggs	2 tbsp lemon juice
½ cup milk	2 tbsp vinegar
2 lbs pears	salt and pepper
grated rind of 1 lemon	

Fry bread in butter until golden. Beat eggs and milk together, pour over bread. Leave until soft. Mix to a paste. Grease a white napkin with butter-put bread mixture in the middle. Gather up the ends and tie tightly together. Put into a pan of boiling water. Simmer for 30 minutes. Peel and slice pears, cook in boiling water for 15 minutes. Add chopped beans and lemon rind. Fry bacon until crisp. Add sugar, lemon juice, vinegar, and pepper and 3 tbsp water. Simmer for 3 minutes. Pour over pears and beans. Simmer for 5 minutes. Strain. Turn dumpling out onto a heated serving platter. Surround with pears and beans.

Fish Dumplings

Fischklösse

½ lb boned raw fish	1 small onion, chopped
1 white bread roll, soaked in water and squeezed dry.	1 egg yolk
	2 tsp chopped parsley
½ cup milk	3 tbsp grated Parmesan cheese
½ stick butter	salt and pepper

Grind fish. Heat butter, saute the onion and bread for 2-3 minutes. Mix with the rest of the ingredients until firm. Break off pieces and shape into large rounds. Roll in flour, cook in boiling salted water for 5-7 minutes. Serve with potato puree and bechamel sauce.

Fish
Dumplings

DUMPLINGS

Frankfurter Pudding

Sachertorte

Frankfurter Pudding

¼ stick butter	½ cup red wine
¼ cup sugar	2 cloves
4 eggs, separated	grated rind of 1 lemon
2 tbsps chopped almonds	pinch ground cinnamon
1 cup soft white breadcrumbs	

Beat egg yolks and sugar together until very light. Add the almonds, cinnamon, breadcrumbs, and 2 tbsps wine. Beat well. Fold in the beaten egg whites. Grease a pudding basin with the butter, sprinkle with sugar. Spoon in the mixture. Cover tightly. Place in a saucepan of boiling water, cover and boil for 1 hour. Bring rest of wine to a boil with the grated lemon rind. Simmer for 5 minutes. Serve over pudding. Serves 6.

Sachertorte

1 stick butter	1 cup grated chocolate
½ cup sugar	2 tbsps apricot jam chocolate
1 cup sifted cake flour	icing
5 eggs, separated	

Beat butter and sugar together. Gradually add flour and egg yolks. Beat well. Add grated chocolate. Beat egg whites until soft peaks form. Fold into chocolate mixture. Pour into a greased and floured 10″ spring form pan. Bake at 350°F for 30 minutes, or until cake tests done. Cool the cake on a rack. When completely cooled, split the cake into two layers. Spread bottom half with apricot jam. Replace the top half, and spread with chocolate icing.

Apple Strudel

Apfelstrudel

6 cups sliced tart apples	½ box (16-oz size) frozen fillo
¾ cup raisins	leaves, thawed*
1 tbsp grated lemon rind	1¾ cups butter or margarine,
¾ cup sugar	melted
2 tsps cinnamon	1 cup fine bread crumbs
¾ cup ground almonds	

Mix apples with raisins, lemon rind, sugar, cinnamon, and almonds. Set aside.

Place 1 fillo leaf on a kitchen towel and brush with melted butter. Place a second leaf on top and brush with butter again. Repeat until 5 leaves have been used, using about ½ cup of butter.

Cook and stir the bread crumbs with ¼ cup butter until lightly browned. Sprinkle ⅜ cup crumbs on the layered fillo leaves.

Mound ½ of the filling in a 3-inch strip along the narrow edge of the fillo, leaving a 2-inch border. Lift towel, using it to roll leaves over apples, jelly-roll fashion. Brush strudel with butter after each turn. Using towel, place strudel on greased baking sheet. Brush top of the strudel with butter and sprinkle with 2 tablespoons crumbs. Repeat the entire procedure for the second strudel. Bake the strudels at 400°F for 20 to 25 minutes, until browned. Serve warm. Makes 2 strudels, 6 to 8 servings each.

*Frozen fillo leaves for strudel can be found at many supermarkets.

Apple
Strudel

SWEETS

Cream Cheese Kuchen

Cream Cheese Kuchen

Quarkkuchen

1 package active dry yeast	*filling*
1/2 tsp salt	3 cups sliced tart apples
4 tbsps sugar	1 tbsp lemon juice
2 to 2 1/2 cups unsifted flour	1 tsp cinnamon
1/4 cup butter or margarine	3/4 cup sugar
1/2 cup milk	2 tbsps flour
1 egg	1/2 lb cream cheese, softened
	1 egg

Mix yeast, salt, 4 tbsps sugar, and 3/4 cup flour.

Add butter to milk. Heat until very warm, 120°F to 130°F. Gradually add milk to flour mixture. Beat for 2 minutes. Add egg and 1/2 cup flour. beat with electric beater on high speed for 2 minutes. Mix in enough flour to form a soft dough. Knead for 5 to 10 minutes, until dought is smooth and elastic. Place in greased bowl and let rise 1 hour, until doubled in bulk. Pat dough into well-greased 10-inch springform pan, pressing 1 1/2 inches up the sides of the pan.

Toss apples with lemon juice, cinnamon, 1/4 cup sugar, and 2 tbsps flour. Arrange in rows on top of dough.

Beat together cream cheese, 1/2 cup sugar, and egg. Spread over apples. Let rise in warm place 1 hour.

Bake at 350°F for 30 minutes. Best when served warm. Makes 1 9-inch cake.

Hazelnut Torte

SWEETS

Hazelnut Torte

Haselnusstorte

5 eggs, separated
¾ cup sugar
6 tbsps water
1¾ cups sifted cake flour
1 tsp baking powder
1½ cups ground hazelnuts
    (filberts) *

1 tsp vanilla
2 tbsps confectioners' sugar
1 cup heavy cream, whipped
fresh strawberries, if desired

Beat the egg yolks and sugar until very light, about 5 minutes. Slowly add the water.

Sift the flour and baking powder together. Mix with 1 cup of the nuts. Fold the flour mixture into the egg yolks.

Beat the egg whites until soft peaks form. Gently fold the beaten whites into the batter. Pour into a greased and floured 10-inch springform pan. Bake at 375°F for 30 minutes or until cake tests done. Cool the cake on a rack. When completely cooled, split the cake into 2 layers.

Fold the vanilla, confectioners' sugar, and remaining ½ cup nuts into the whipped cream. Spread whipped cream between the 2 cake layers and on top of the cake. Chill until serving time.

Garnish with fresh strawberries, if desired. Makes 8 servings.

*Hazelnuts are available at speciality or gourmet stores. They should be blanched. To blanch, boil the nuts 5 minutes and, when cool enough to handle, remove the skins. To grind, place about ¼ cup at a time in a blender, or chop finely.

Vanilla Bavarian Cream

Kugelhupf

Vanilla Bavarian Cream

Bayerische Vanillecreme

2 packages unflavoured gelatin	2 eggs, beaten
½ cup cold water	1½ cup milk, scalded
9 tbsps sugar	1 cup vanilla ice cream
1 tbsp cornstarch	1 tsp vanilla
	1 cup heavy cream, whipped

Sprinkle gelatin over cold water to soften. Heat to dissolve gelatin completely.

Mix together sugar and cornstarch. Add eggs; beat for 2 minutes. Slowly add warm milk, beating constantly. Pour into a 1-quart saucepan. Cook over medium heat until custard coats a spoon. Add gelatin and ice cream while custard is hot. Cool until slightly thickened. Add vanilla. Fold in whipped cream. Pour into 1-quart mold. Chill until set.

Unmold carefully and served garnished with fresh fruit. Makes 6 to 8 servings.

Kugelhupf

1 package active dry yeast	rind of 1 lemon, grated
1 cup milk, scalded and cooled	¾ cup raisins
1 cup sugar	⅓ cup ground almonds (2 oz package)
1 cup butter or margarine	½ tsp salt
5 eggs	4 cups unsifted flour
1 tsp vanilla	

Sprinkle yeast in milk to dissolve.

In a large bowl beat sugar and butter until light and fluffy. Beat in eggs, one at a time. Stir in vanilla, lemon rind, raisins, and almonds.

Mix salt and flour. Add milk and flour mixture alternately, ending with flour.

Grease a Kugelhupf mould*, bundt pan, or tube pan. Pour batter into pan. Cover and let rise until doubled in bulk, about 2 hours.

Bake in preheated 375°F oven for 40 minutes, until browned and done. Serve warm with butter. Makes 8 to 10 servings.

*This bread is traditionally baked in a Kugelhupf pan or turban-head pan. If these are unavailable, a bundt pan or tube pan works just as well.

Fresh Fruit Flummery

Fische Obst Flammeri

1 cup semolina	1 cup raspberry puree
2 cups milk	2 egg whites
½ cup sugar	

Bring milk to a boil. Add semolina. Cook for 15 minutes stirring all the time. Add sugar. When thickened remove from heat, fold in raspberry puree then beaten egg whites. Chill before serving.

Fresh Fruit Flummery

SWEETS

Black Forest Cherry Cake

Black Forest Cherry Cake

Schwarzwälder Kirschtorte

6 eggs
1 cup sugar
1 tsp vanilla
4 squares unsweetened
   baking chocolate, melted
1 cup sifted flour

syrup
¼ cup sugar
⅓ cup water
2 tbsps kirsch

filling
1½ cups confectioners' sugar

⅓ cup unsalted butter
1 egg yolk
2 tbsps kirsch liquer

topping
2 cups drained, canned sour
   cherries
2 tbsps confectioners' sugar
1 cup heavy cream, whipped
8-oz bar semisweet chocolate
   bar

Beat eggs, sugar, and vanilla together until thick and fluffy, about 10 minutes. Alternately fold chocolate and flour into the egg mixture, ending with flour.

Pour the batter into 3 8-inch round cake pans that have been well-greased and floured. Bake in a preheated 350°F oven 10 to 15 minutes, until a cake tester inserted in center comes out clean. Cool cakes in pans 5 minutes; turn out on racks to cool completely.

Make syrup by mixing together sugar and water and boiling for 5 minutes. When syrup has cooled, stir in kirsch.

Prick the cake layers and pour syrup over all 3 layers.

To make the butter-cream filling. Beat together sugar and butter until well-blended. Add egg yolk; beat until light and fluffy, about 3 to 5 minutes. Fold in kirsch.

To assemble cake, place 1 layer on cake plate. Spread with the butter-cream filling.

Using ¾ cup cherries, which have been patted dry, drop cherries evenly over cream. Place second layer on cake. Repeat. Place third layer on top.

Fold 2 tbsps confectioners' sugar into whipped cream. Cover sides and top of cake with wipped cream. Decorate top of cake with remaning ½ cup cherries.

To make chocolate curls from chocolate bar, shave bar (at room temperature) with vegetable peeler. Refrigerate curls until ready to use. Press chocolate curls on sides of cake and sprinkle a few on top. Chill until serving time. Makes 8 to 10 servings.

Apple Cake

SWEETS

Apple Cake

Blitzkuchen mit Äpfeln

4 to 6 tart apples (medium size)
2 lemons, juiced
3 tbsps sugar
3 tbsps butter
¾ cup sugar
2 egg yolks (do not put 2 yolks together, as they will be used individually)
½ lemon, juiced and peel grated

1 tsp baking powder
1½ cups flour
¾ cup milk
1 tbsp rum
2 egg whites
1 tsp butter (to grease cake pan)
1 tsp vegetable oil
3 tbsps powdered sugar

Peel apples, cut in half, and core. Cut decorative lengthwise slits in apples, about ½ inch deep (see picture). Sprinkle with lemon juice and sugar. Set aside.

Cream butter and sugar together. One at a time, beat in egg yolks. Gradually beat in lemon juice and grated peel.

Sift baking powder and flour together. Gradually add to batter. Blend in milk and rum. In a small bowl beat egg whites until stiff. Fold into batter.

Generously grease a springform pan. Pour in batter and top with apple halves. Brush apples with oil. Bake in preheated 350°F oven 35 to 40 minutes.

Remove from pan and sprinkle with powdered sugar. Makes 6 servings.

INDEX

The publishers would like to express their thanks to GROSVENOR HOUSE for kindly providing the facilities for photography, and to ROLF ELSNER, Senior executive Chef of Grosvenor House, for preparing the dishes. Photography by Neil Sutherland.

First published in Great Britain 1983 by Colour Library Books Ltd.
© 1983 Illustrations and text: Colour Library Books Ltd. Guildford, Surrey, England.
Photoset by The Printed Word Ltd. London, England.
Colour separations by Reprocolor Llovet, S.A.
Printed by Cayfosa, bound by Eurobinder in Barcelona, Spain
All rights reserved.
ISBN 0-86283-100-8
COLOUR LIBRARY BOOKS